Set Free From Satanic Bondage

(The Confession Of A Former Devil Worshipper)

By

Ledia Tumelo Ramodipa

i

Set Free From Satanic Bondage

Approved
By
Blessed Thabang Mobosi

Set Free From Satanic Bondage

Set Free From Satanic Bondage

Published by

William Jenkins
2503-4288 Grange Street
Burnaby BC V5H 1P2 Canada

williamhenryjenkins@gmail.com
http://williamjenkins.ca
Telephone: 1-604-685-4136
Cell: 1-778-953-6139

Written by

Ledia Tumelo Ramodipa
Letaba, Limpopo Province
0870
South Africa

lediaramodipa@gmail.com

Edition 1

ISBN: 978-1-928164-19-7

Set Free From Satanic Bondage

Dedication

I dedicate this book to my heavenly father, the Father of our Lord Jesus Christ, the God of my salvation who delivered me from the Kingdom of Darkness and brought me back safe to the Kingdom of his dear son, where I was redeemed and my sins were forgiven.

Set Free From Satanic Bondage

Acknowledgement

I give my thanks to my parents, Pastor Mr. Ramodipa and Mrs. Ramodipa. Thanks for your encouragement and help throughout my life.

I also thank Apostle Noel for being available to me throughout my deliverance process.

Set Free From Satanic Bondage

Contents

Set Free From Satanic Bondage

Author Ledia Tumelo Ramodipa

Μy name is Ledia Ramodipa. My mother carried me in her womb for 10 months until I was born on the 30 July 1993 at Sehlakong, South Africa. I was born into and grew up in a Christian family.

I am currently living with my family; my dad and mom, as well with my two younger sisters, my two younger brothers and my daughter. I am studying electrical engineering.

Set Free From Satanic Bondage

I grew up loving to sing together with my family and we would sing every night before going to bed.

As well, I am an instrumentalist. My favorite musical instrument is the guitar, which I play the most often.

I have a cry in my spirit, a wish that all the people who serve Darkness, after reading this book, may be delivered from Satan and take their place in life in Jesus' Name.

Introduction

We are in the end times and the Devil is ruling the lives of many people. Many people are unaware that the world is coming to an end and that Jesus Christ is coming, not soon, but right away. The Devil knows that God created Hell for him and his angels, as well for those who follow him. He knows that his time is up and that he is about to be taken to the pit of Hell where he belongs. He doesn't want to go there alone.

"Then I saw an angel coming down from heaven with the key of the bottomless pit (Hell) and a heaven chain in his hand. He seized the dragon - that old serpent who is called the Devil, Satan - and bound him in chains for a thousand years. The angel threw him into the bottomless pit, which he then shut and locked so that Satan will deceive the nations no more. **Revelations 20:1-2 (NLT)**

The Devil wants to cause you to rebel against God and his ways so that you will be cast into Hell with him. He is carrying on his activity by making people remain under his authority so that when they die, they will go to hell. As well, when Rapture takes place, many will be left behind.

In this book I will describe how I joined the Kingdom of Darkness where the Devil, Lucifer, is the King without mercy. As well, I will tell you how I got out of his influence.

God exists; the Devil exists; Jesus exists; Lucifer and the rebellious Angels exist. As well, demons, evil spirits, the Holy Spirit, and angels of the true God exist.

As you read my story you will become aware of the strategies of the Devil and his Darkness Kingdom.

Be blessed as you read.

How I Joined the Kingdom of Darkness

In 2005 when I was doing my Grade 6, in my sleep I was always dreaming of seeing myself driving a car. I thought it was just a dream. One night I woke up at around 2:30 a.m. and found myself in bushes. I remember screaming, but no one was there to help or who could hear me. I heard a voice laughing at me as I was screaming for help.

I began to run, trying to find a way back home. I didn't know what was going on with me. In the morning when I awoke, I found myself at home in my bed. My clothes were torn apart and many thorns were under my feet.

I wanted to tell my parents, but I couldn't because I easily forgot what had happened in the dream. Later on, my dream changed to another one. I started dreaming seeing myself drinking juice and eating human flesh. In the morning, I could smell my hands and mouth smelling as if I were holding rotten meat.

Eating the meat and eating human flesh were part of the initiation into the Kingdom of Darkness and showed, as well, how I was supposed to live after the initiation. The juice is not actual juice; it is human blood.

At first, they'll tell you it's blood and it would appear to be blood in the dream, but you'll be drinking blood.

This dream happened repeatedly until November 2005. I can still remember it as though it happened yesterday.

In December 2005, on the 20th, I was asleep at home. When I woke up at around 12 midnight, I suddenly started speaking in a strange language that I couldn't understand. I couldn't control myself and I just continued to speak like that.

Then, I heard a loud, bold voice saying, "It's time to go".

I was terrified; my heart was filled with fear. Trembling, I asked the voice, "Where are we going"?

I could hear the voice speaking, but I couldn't see who was speaking. Sometimes I could see scary creatures that I had never seen before.

The voice said, "Close Your Eyes" so I did. After a while when I opened my eyes, I found myself in a large place like a stadium where I saw people gathered together according to their race: blacks,

Indians, whites and other races. Some of these people were wearing a long black dress with a black hat and others were in a long red dress with a red hat.

They were no lights in that place. It was dark and only a dim light. At the entrance of the gate I saw two people who were holding spears and, in the middle of the gate, I saw a very big dragon. As I looked at the gate, it opened. Then, I felt a cold wind. While it was like that, I felt something entering my body.

Then I heard a voice from somewhere in that place saying, "Welcome".

I tried to look around to see where the voice was coming from, but I saw nothing. When I looked backward, I saw two creatures. Both of these creatures appeared to have two heads, that of a human in the front and that of a snake at the back.

As I looked at these two creatures, they pointed up at a board where was written "semiya labussa bayada". It means "welcome to my world". At the bottom was written, "DQ", which stands for "Devil's Queue".

When I saw that, I fell down and started crying very hard. Then, one of my teachers who was teaching at the school I was attending came by. He said, "Stop crying because it won't help". He looked into my eyes for a period of time.

A few minutes later, that place disappeared and I found myself in my bedroom. By then, it was about 4:30 in the morning. I was confused and tears were all over me. I didn't know what was happening to me. I was trying to figure it out.

As well, I didn't tell my parents of my experience. Unwarily, I had been initiated into the Kingdom of Darkness.

Devilish Operations through the Dreams
In 2006, I had a dream wherein I saw myself in a graveyard. At this graveyard, there were no graves, but only holes that had been dug. There were many of these holes and I found it to be scary. I was trembling and terrified as well as astonished.

Then, I saw two men with long red gowns who were standing far away from me. Suddenly, they came to where I was. The first man had two heads, a head of a human being and a head of a dragon. The other one had one human head, but he had long sharp teeth and long grey hair. The one with two heads said, "If you can fill these empty holes with human bodies, the car that you've been driving in the dream can be yours in reality".

He meant that I could have the car physically in the real world. He gave me a bowl of blood and asked me to drink it and so I did. The men took my hands and placed them upon theirs. They started to speak in some satanic language or, let me say, in satanic chants and incantations.

While they were chanting, there started to be lightning everywhere. My body started to vibrate as if I were getting electrical shocks. I fell down and couldn't control myself anymore.

I started to do bad things. I felt happy when people were fighting. I could dream of killing someone only to find out that in reality I had killed the person. Overall, I was thinking that all that happened was just dreams. However, I found out that everything was reality. The killings were truly happening in the real world.

How I Realized that I was Initiated as a Devil Worshipper

In 2007, I was in a church where I attended a youth conference. In the front where the church pulpit was placed, I saw the strange creatures that I had once seen previously. They were standing next to the pastor and waving their hands at me. I looked at a brother next to me and he said, "I see them also". He was so happy to see those creatures.

I then realized that Satanism does exist in some churches; that some churches are under the authority of Satan.

I was expecting those creatures to appear again because they were not too clear to me. Around 1:30 a.m., I felt my body was changing. There started to be a formation of tattoos all over my body and the mark of 666 on my right hand.

He required everyone great and small, rich and the poor, slave or free to be given the mark of the forehead or on the right hand and no one could sell or buy anything without the mark 666, which was the name of the beast or the number representing his name. Wisdom is needed to understand this. Let the one with understanding solve the number of the beast, for its number its 666. **Revelations 13:16.**

After the formation of the tattoos and the mark of the 666, I felt something moving up and down on my left hand. I then saw a tattoo of a cross that is opposite to the one used when Jesus was crucified. It was the opposite cross. On my thigh, I saw two tattoos of snakes that moved up and down. Their heads could go up off my skin. When this happened, blood would come out of my skin through their heads.

Suddenly I felt something moving up and down on my stomach. I felt weak and dizzy and I couldn't shout for help. Then, those creatures I had seen, appeared to me physically. They sat on my bed. I asked them who they were. They just laughed terribly.

The one with two heads said, "My name is Manasseh". The second one said, "My name is Khadukeh". They explained why they had come. They said, "You have being chosen by the Shining One". The Shining One is the interpretation of the name "Lucifer", the name that God gave Satan when he was created before he became a rebel in heaven.

"Well", I asked, "Who is he"?

They said I shouldn't ask. They said that he has chosen me and that I was so important to him.

I asked "Why me"? and they just said "Because you are smart".

Then Khadukeh said I must not be afraid of those tattoos on my body, that they were to protect me and to hide me. He said that no one would see them except me alone. He said that the conversation between them and me must be a secret and that if I told anyone about this, I would die. Then, they disappeared.

What was my service in the Kingdom of Darkness?

In 2008, I became very dangerous. I started killing people by causing accidents. I was able to point at a car with a single finger and the car would lose control resulting in an accident.

All these things happened physically. Spiritually, it was just a backup.

As well, I was able to possess people and make them join the Kingdom of Darkness unwarily.

In 2009, I was pastoring a school-based student Christian Organization that I belonged to. We were a mixture of Christians from different churches with different pastors with different teaching and different ways in which things were conducted in their churches. It wasn't that easy for anyone to know that I was operating by the power of Darkness since the organization was run by young learners.

The other genuine Christians were still young spiritually, i.e. not yet matured spiritually to discern who I was.

I was 16 years old, had my own part-time ministry and conducted my own services after school.

During school holidays I would do revivals and crusades.

In my ministry, I was using the water that I got in the Devil's Queue (DQ). The Devil's Queue is under the sea. My ex-bosses gave it to me under the sea in the Darkness Kingdom. Dead people were using this water to bathe. Some of this water was also used in the mortuary. Those who served the Kingdom of Darkness who work in the mortuary would use this water to wash the corpse and return the water back to the Devil's Queue (DQ), where the water comes from.

We were ordained to go and possess people in churches. They gave us that water to sprinkle on people when praying for them while I spoke in satanic language. People would think I was speaking in the heavenly languages of the holy angels of God, but I wasn't. The words were not from the Holy Spirit, but satanic language.

Many people would come for prayer. The more I sprinkled that water on them, the more they were possessed and connected with Darkness. Falling down was a confirmation that you caught the spirit that was in that water and a sign that you now belonged to the Kingdom of Darkness. I was also giving DQ water to pastors to use in their churches.

15

I killed many people. Those holes that I was told to fill with human bodies were becoming filled. For that reason I was promoted in the Kingdom of Darkness. As a promotion, I was ordained as the leader of the Devil worshippers around the town where I was staying. As a leader, I started giving my converts missions to complete. I got stronger, more powerful and more dangerous every day. I had many powers. I could change to be a snake, a sea fish, a sea horse, an ant, a grasshopper or anything that I wanted to be. As well, I could be invisible.

My Possessions in Darkness

In March, 2009, I received a very big house with eleven rooms, a car (a Hammer NH3), lots of clothes, jewelry and money. There was a limit to the amount of money, but I had enough.

I was married to a pastor who was having a ministry. He didn't know that I was married to him and that I was his spiritual wife. His ministry experienced failure because he was married to a Devil worshipper.

Incidentally, I was using a Satanic bible, the one that is written opposite the true Holy Bible that God wrote through his Holy Spirit using his servants. I will tell you about it later.

Regarding the car and the house, I had them in real life even though I was only sixteen years old. I used to give a ride to some learners on the way to school. They didn't know that the car and house were the product of Darkness. They just knew me as a preacher and a good person.

As for my parents, I was a rebel against them. I wasn't staying with them. I just went away. They were concerned about the house and car issue. There was nothing they could do about it because I would ignore whatever they said. They only thing they did was to pray for me because I was a rebel against them.

A Covenant I made with Satan

One day while I was sleeping, Manasseh and Khadukeh came to me and told me that I did a great job in their Kingdom. They told me that we are going somewhere; they meant to the Devils Queue (DQ). We disappeared and appeared there.

When we entered, I saw a stage in the middle of this place. It was like a very big stadium. There was a podium with three chairs. On the middle chair, there was a dragon.

He seized the dragon, that ancient serpent, who is the devil, or Satan, and bound him for a thousand years. **Revelations 20:2.**

On the chair that was on left hand side, I saw a creature with three heads, a head of a dragon, a head of a human and a head a snake. The chair on the right hand side had no one on it, but on it were a red gown and a book. While I stood there, Manasseh said that the third chair on the right hand side was mine. I was astonished. While I was still astonished, Manasseh told me that I had to go and kill my mother and my father.

Well! I went to a mirror and spoke, "Mirror mirror, show me". I said that twice. The third time I spoke, my parents appeared on the mirror. I could observe them on the screen. They were covered by something that was like glass.

Manasseh shouted at me, "Quickly, Angelina, go". (Angelina was my name in the Kingdom of Darkness.) I disappeared from the Devil's Queue and appeared in my parents' room. I hit my dad with lightning on his head. He was supposed to die, but he didn't die because of the glass-like thing that was shielding him. Suddenly, he woke up and called the name of Jesus. I lost balance and my powers could not prevail upon him. I couldn't stand that name. I disappeared back to the DQ.

I told Manasseh that my power couldn't prevail against my father, and, as well, that he was so difficult to kill.

As you know, the Devil is a king without mercy. I was beaten badly because I couldn't prevail in killing my parents. After my punishment, Manasseh told me that there are other groups who are leaders of the Shining One (Satan). Then Manasseh told me that they failed to accomplish some of their given missions that the Shining One told them to accomplish. He told me that they are going to be punished by me as I've being punished. He gave me a big chain that had some flames of fire burning all over it.

After that he asked me if I could see the person sitting in the middle chair of those three chairs with shining around him. I told him "I don't see any shining thing; I see just a dragon".

He slapped me and told me to bow down to the dragon.

He said, "That is the Shining One". He said, "You're lucky that he chose you for his Kingdom".

"The seventy returned with joy, saying, "Lord, even the demons are subject to us in Your name." And He said to them, "I was watching Satan fall from heaven like lightning. "Behold, I have given you authority to tread on serpents and scorpions, and over all the power of the enemy, and nothing will injure you. "
Luke 10:17-19.

Then I asked, "Who is the one sitting on the left hand side"?

He said, "He is the grandchild of the Shining One. His name is Lusindra", meaning the grandchild of Lucifer. The third chair on the right hand of the Shining One (Satan) with a red gown on it and a book was for me.

Manasseh took the red gown and put it on me and also gave me the book. This meant that I was crowned as the Queen of the Kingdom of Darkness as well as the wife of Lucifer. On the book it was written, "Brillo Celeste". This is a satanic language statement that means "Holy Bible", but in a satanic way.

On top of the cover page of that book was an inverted cross with a snake on it. The Satanic Bible is written with messages opposite to the true Holy Bible. I took it along with me and Manasseh told me that there is no other bible as powerful as that. Then he took me to another room.

In this strange room, I saw many people that I thought were dead. Some of them were my family members. I also saw the teacher who used to teach me at school. He was correcting the learner script there in the Kingdom of Darkness. I saw the names of the learners I knew on some of the script he was marking. This teacher was teaching in the same school I was attending. He was also a Devil worshipper.

We passed to another room where I saw dead bodies hanging by chains. We passed to another room where I saw people who seemed not to be normal humans or creatures. They made me think of aliens. Some of these creatures did not have complete ears; others had one eye and two ears. For others, their mouth was on the cheek and they had sharp, yellowish-brownish teeth. Their garments were filthy and torn apart like rags. These creatures were cutting human bodies with machines and sharp knives. I also saw some children who were carrying buckets of water entering the room.

From there we went outside the room. There was lightning everywhere and it was scary. Manasseh started making some satanic incantations, chants and singing.

Then there appeared this big snake with seven heads. Manasseh grabbed me. We sat on the snake and it flew to a big river. Next to the river, I saw people who I recognized who were selling human parts such as intestines, livers, human heads, tongues, breasts, private parts and human blood in bottles, etc. I was terrified and started to cry. The snake went deep inside the river.

I was in another world in that river. I saw what I've never seen before. I saw two beautiful ladies who were like fish. We left the river and came across some shops.

Well! It seemed real to me. These shops were selling clothes and shoes. Some of the stores were manufacturers of these shoes and clothes. I walked around the shops to observe everything. I went to another room where I saw people designing, but I couldn't see their faces. They were wearing long red gowns. Their work was to manufacture those clothes and shoes.

On a wall I saw designer T-shirts with writing on them:
1. **DIVA**
   -**D**- Devil
   -**I**- In
   -**V**-Victory
   -**A**- Always
2. **MISSY**
   -**M**-Me
   -**I**-In
   -**s**-Slavery
   -**S**-Same
   -**Y**-Year

3. **RAP**
   -**R**-Rest
   -**A**-Again
   -**P**-Politely

4. **BAD BOYS**

-**B**-Blood
-**A**-And
-**D**-Danger
-**B**-Boy
-**O**-On
-**Y**-You
-**S**-Shame

I only remember those ones for now, but there were many on that wall that day. There were even different animal drawings including that of a snake. I was shocked and, at the same time, crying for people who go to the wrong shops to buy these clothes and shoes that are designed by the Kingdom of Darkness. Some shops that sell clothes and shoes as well as food belong to the Kingdom of Darkness, and their products are used to possess people and initiate them into the Kingdom of Darkness unaware.

Some shop owners belong to the Kingdom of Darkness. Some of these shop owners are not human beings; they are demons. The Angels of Darkness can manifest in human form. If you buy their product, especially if you're not a Christian, you become one of them after wearing it.

We went to the next room where they were designing jewelry and selling it. The jewelry had some animals on them. Some had a pyramid sign.

Manasseh said there was one thing that I needed to see before we go. We entered a big building. In it I saw pastors whom I knew. Their churches had various names. I saw a pastor of a ministry called The Twelve Apostles. I saw a pastor of Z.C.C. (Zion Christian Church). I also saw a pastor of I.P.C.C. whose ministry name has changed to I.P.H., the International Pentecostal Church. I also saw a pastor of Jehovah's Witness. I saw Indians and their gods; I saw Chinese and their gods; I saw sangomas and fortune tellers (psychiatrists).

I also saw some teachers who were teaching in the school where I was attending. I asked why all those people were in there. Manasseh said, "They belong to the Kingdom of Darkness and they are serving there to recruit people to the Kingdom of Darkness".

I was surprised because there were also some people who call themselves pastors as well as prophets that are on the television with mega churches. These people pretend to be men of God or servant of the most high God, whereas they are not. They are the Angels of Darkness. Many people love these pastors and prophets. They attend their services and crusades not knowing that they are Angels of Darkness.

I started to feel sorry for those people who go to the pastors and prophets who pretend to be the servant of the True God, the father of my Lord and Savior, Jesus Christ. It doesn't matter which church you attend. The question is who is in authority in that church, Satan or Jesus? What I know is that there are only two Kingdoms namely: the Kingdom of Darkness that is for Lucifer, the rebellious angel whom the true Holy Bible calls the dragon, the old serpent, the Devil Satan; and the Kingdom of Light that is the Kingdom of God's dear son Jesus Christ. Which Kingdom has dominion in your church and your house?

All sinners belong to the Kingdom of Darkness. As the bible says, he that is a sinner belongs to Satan. Only genuine born-again Christians who have accepted Jesus Christ as their Lord and Savior and who have genuinely repented of their sins will enter the Kingdom of Heaven, the Kingdom of the Light.

While I was still in that building, Manasseh took a sharp knife and cut himself into two pieces. I was trembling. He pointed at me. I felt my body changing. My body was separated into two halves.

Manasseh's half bonded with mine and my other half bonded with his. While our bodies were bonding they repositioned themselves into our actual body shape.

Manasseh started to speak with the satanic language. I started shaking as if I was struck by electricity. Manasseh told me to cut myself because he needed blood.

For the life of a creature is in the blood, and I have given it to you to make atonement for yourselves on the alter; it is the blood that makes atonement for one's life. **Leviticus 17:11**

Manasseh drank my blood and I drank his. He then told me that we were no longer two but one. That was a blood covenant. That was a long night.

How I was serving Satan at school and in churches

As time went by, I forgot that I was a Devil worshipper due to the fact that everything was just normal. In 2009, one day while I was at school where I was doing my high school level, they started a Student Christian Organization (S.C.O.). As I was from a Christian family, I loved going to church. While in the class where I attended the S.C.O., I sang a song that says, "I'm going home".

Unusual things started to happen. As I sang, some learners fell down. Those from Z.C.C. started to prophecy. Miracles, signs and wonders took place. In a short while I heard Manasseh saying, "That Book, take it and preach".

He was referring to that Satanic Bible. I didn't even delay. I went to the front holding that Satanic Bible and started to preach. While I preached from that bible, things became worse. Learners were falling, some were manifesting miracles, signs and wonders that are unimaginable were taking place.

At this time, I thought that it was the Holy Spirit working through me, and when the voice of Manasseh spoke to me, I thought it was God. Actually, I was preaching under the influence of an evil spirit that was working through me. It was the power of the Kingdom of Darkness that was working by then.

As well, I could preach in churches and the same thing would happen. People would think I was used by God whereas it was Darkness. It takes only a genuine Christian with a true discerning spirit to differentiate the spirit that comes from God or Satan. For this purpose it is important for Christians to have the discerning spirit so that they can differentiate the activities that are from God from those that are not from God.

How I was Delivered from The Kingdom Of Darkness

How God anointed Jesus of Nazareth with the Holy Ghost and power, and how he went about doing good, and healing all who were under the power of the devil, because God was with him. **Acts 10:38.**

In 2010 I was doing grade 10 for the second time. This time I had told myself that I wanted to quit Devil worshipping and be a normal person again. I wasn't enjoying myself anymore. In June 2010, I fasted and prayed hard to God so that he could deliver me from the satanic bondage.

Truly, I tell you, there is no joy in Satan. He is happy to see people in all forms of bondage. There is nothing that the Devil can offer or do other than to steal, to kill and to destroy. Even if you're serving him, your destiny is to accomplish those three missions and the missions will take place in your life as well. He will use you and later kill you. If not, he will just steal from you or destroy you and abandon you. The Devil is a king without mercy.

As I continued fasting, nothing happened. Remember, no one goes to the father (God the creator, the most high God who is the true God above all) except through Jesus Christ. If you have not accepted Jesus as your personal Lord and savior, even if you pray, you're a stranger in his sight. You're still a sinner and you're under the dominion of Satan. You become redeemed only by accepting Jesus as your Lord and savior and by genuinely repenting your sins. Jesus is the key or let me say, the ticket, to appear before the almighty God.

I was like that. There was no mark or sign of Jesus in my life. As my soul and spirit were in the Kingdom of Darkness, I needed deliverance and I didn't give on the fasting. Nothing happened because by then I didn't have the knowledge that I had to accept Jesus first to take away my burdens. As he said, *"Come to me all you who are weary and burdened and I will give you rest."* **Matthew 11:28.**

In July 2010, my ex-bosses Manasseh and Khadukeh came to me. They told me that I would be sorry if I leave their Kingdom.

In the morning of the following day, I woke up with the manifestation of those tattoos on my body. On the head of the snake tattoos, blood was coming out through its mouth. The snakes were real physically. The drawings were not just drawings, but actually snakes.

I bled continually. I took a needle and pricked the head of those snakes, then used a bandage to cover my thigh. I went to school, but while I was in the classroom the bleeding continued. This time it was worse. I ran back home straight to my room.

While I was in my room, my ex-boss appeared to me and said, "I told you you'll be sorry for trying to leave our Kingdom".

He then insisted that he would stop the bleeding only if I would go to Venda to kill Pastor Irene Tshifiwa. He said that Pastor Irene is threatening the Kingdom of Darkness and destroying the works of the Devil as well.

Pastor Irene is the founder of World Restoration Service By Jesus Christ (WRS). She exposes the works of Darkness and destroys them. You can watch her Television program on the DSTV public Channels (WRS). I agreed to go and kill her because I wanted the bleeding to stop.

I came up with a plan to go there. I went with my friend who was also a servant in the Kingdom of Darkness. We arrived late and found a place where we could rest a bit. Early in the morning, we went to a church in a place called Manini located in Venda. Venda is located in Limpopo province in South Africa.

When we arrived in that church (CWC), Pastor Irene Tshifiwa came in. I looked straight into her eyes trying to attack her to death with the powers that were in my eyes. Instead, I was arrested by the power of the Almighty God.

I remember running back and fro. There was too much power over which I could not prevail. I fell down. I was powerless.

I couldn't stand and felt something coming out of my feet. It was the needle that was under the flesh of my feet. The needle was to prevent the snake in my body from coming out. It came out of my leg.

It was a long day. I was arrested by the Angels of God. I was prayed over, but the game was not yet over. The following day I confessed since I saw that I was losing the battle. As the bible says, *"People who conceal their sins will not prosper, but if they confess and turn from them, they will receive mercy"*. **Proverbs 28:13**.

After I was exposed there as one of Darkness, I confessed. Pastor Irene asked me if I wanted to repent and come to the Kingdom of the Light to Jesus or to remain under Darkness? She preached to me and showed me the Light and I accepted to surrender my Life to Jesus. Then she prayed for me.

As I was deep in Darkness, my deliverance did not occur in one day. It took three days to deliver me and these days were not consecutive. On the second last day before the last day of my final deliverance, I was sleeping when I heard a very big, strange sound in my room. I woke up suddenly. The light in my room was turned off. I saw a person wearing a linen cloth standing in front of me. I was unable to see the face of this person because his face was too bright, shining with a bright light. I could see only his hands and feet.

He said to me, "Do not be afraid. I am not here to hurt you. I am going with you back to the DQ, but today will be different. We are going there, but not in the same way you did previously".

He was Archangel Michael. He told me to close my eyes and when I did, we appeared in the DQ. When we arrived at the gate of the DQ, he told me to go in and collect that book, the Satanic Bible, so that it can be destroyed.

While I walked in, I remembered when King David said in his psalm that, *"Even though I walk through the darkest valley, I will fear no evil, for you are with me; your rod and your staff, they comfort me."* **Psalm 23.**

As I walked in, I saw the Angels of Darkness (Demons). These demons were holding spears and were wearing long black gowns.

As I walked forward towards where the book sat on my former chair on the right hand side of Lucifer, one of the demons struck me with a spear. I started to bleed a great deal. Lusindra took me and placed me on my chair at the right hand side of Satan. They bound me with chains to a point where I was unable to do anything. By this time Archangel Michael was at the door. I started crying thinking that I was going to die.

After few minutes I remembered what Apostle Paul said.
" but despite all this, overwhelming victory is ours through Christ who loved us enough to die for us. For I am convinced that nothing can ever separate us from his love. Death can't, and life can't. The angels won't, and all the powers of hell itself cannot keep God's love away. Our fears for today, our worries about tomorrow, or where we are—high above the sky, or in the deepest ocean— nothing will ever be able to separate us from the love of God demonstrated by our Lord Jesus Christ when he died for us. **Romans 8:37-39.**

Before I entered, Michael had told me that I must come back to where he was. He didn't go inside with me because he wanted to see whether or not I was going to run inside and not come back. He told me that if I don't return to him, they will kill me. As well, he wanted to see that was I determined to leave Darkness.

After my meditations of that verse from Apostle Paul, fear left me and I regained my faith. Remember, fear is the opposite of faith. As God is pleased by faith, so is Satan pleased by fear. The only place where Satan can operate is where there is fear. So, after I regained my faith, Michael appeared and pointed a sword at me. The chains fell off me. I then started singing a song that says, "I lay my life on you".

Archangel Michael grabbed me with his hand. We were not walking on the surface of that place; we were sliding on the atmosphere going out of that place. We got out of that place while Michael was speaking in Heavenly languages. He took me straight home to my room and placed me on my bed.

I don't know how all that happened. It was just miraculous. My eyes were closed for a while and opened when I was on my bed. While I sat there on my bed, Michael was standing next to me holding my hand.

In my other hand I was holding the Satanic Bible. There was fire all over it, but it wasn't burning me. The hole where I was struck by a spear by that demon was so painful. Michael prayed for me. The hole became closed and disappeared just like that.

He then said to me, "If you go back, you'll die young and go to hell".

From that time, I was delivered from Darkness.

As for the book, I took it to Pastor Irene at CWC where she was ministering at that time. I don't know what they did with it. I left the book there. I think they burned it because that's what they usually do to the tools of Darkness.

Satan was one of God's angels in heaven as well as the leader of one of his armies. He and all the angels that followed him in the rebellion against God were part of God's created order before they were cast from heaven and fell to earth and became evil spirits. Lucifer, the former angel of God who is now Satan, the serpent, as well as the dragon, along with the rebellious angels who followed him, opposed God's rule of the universe.

Satan, who is the god of this evil world, has made him blind, unable to see the glorious light of the Gospel that is shining upon him or to understand the amazing message we preach about the glory of Christ, who is the image of God.
2 Corinthians 4:4.

They influence people who haven't received Jesus Christ as their Lord and savior, but those who have accepted him have gratitude because Jesus Christ destroyed their power over his people. Now Jesus Christ has set me free. Jesus Christ has set me free from the power of Satan and death has no power over my life.

For he has rescued us out of the darkness and gloom of Satan's kingdom and brought us into the Kingdom of his dear Son, who bought our freedom with his blood and forgave us all our sins.
Colossians 1:13-14.

What Happened after my Deliverance

After my deliverance, things were very tough for me. It was not easy at all. In 2010, I passed grade 10 very well even though it wasn't easy. I remember sometimes my classmates didn't want to write exams or tests with me sitting next to them. Even the person invigilating us would request me to go and write outside sitting under a tree.

I remember one day when I was requested to stay outside. The rain began to fall. I was wet and cold at the same time. When I submitted my script, they just tore it apart. With my life being so hard like that I strengthened myself by the word of God.

"So be strong and courageous, all you who put your hope in the Lord". **Psalm 31:24.**

In 2011 I went to grade 11. My classmates were very afraid of me and had a problem with me. They would run away from me when they saw me or they would take actions to avoid me when they saw me coming. They didn't want to sit close to me or talk to me.

In the place where I was living, the people were threatening to kill me accusing me of being a witch. Some parents started to take their children out of the school to another school to avoid their children being in my company. Two weeks after all these occurrences, I decided to drop out of school for the sake of other learners whose parents were taking them out of the school because of me.

I was concerned especially for those who were doing matric that year because it was not possible for them to be removed to another school. I left school with a mentality of loving the innocent learners and innocent teachers, as well as my friends. I wanted not to be the cause of their destruction. I wanted to give them the opportunity to focus on their studies; I wanted to avoid any opportunity they would have of being afraid of me.

I dropped out of school discouraged and disheartened. I was a good student, highly performing at school, but that was the choice I made due to confusion and rejection that I experienced.

Due to all that, I was not having peace in my life. I thought of committing suicide. At that time I thought that death was the only solution to my pains.

After my deliverance life wasn't easy at all, not even for a single day. Things were just getting worse every day. I remember one day when I closed my room door to pray asking God to take away my spirit. The hatred and rejection that I experienced from the community was just too much. I couldn't cope anymore. I lost my patience, hope and faith as well. I sorrowfully said to myself that nothing good would ever come out of my life.

As time went on, I found myself in fellowship with a woman by the name of Prophetess Dinah who has a church in Tzaneen. She got my history and welcomed me with open arms. I was welcome in her home and she treated me like one of her own children.

In July 2011, the Devil came back to me. He asked me if I had forgotten the blood covenant that I had made with Manasseh. At this moment, I was in front of the mirror, sitting down, combing my hair, preparing to go to church. As I looked into the mirror the image reflected into two and I saw the images of me and of Manasseh. He was smiling. When I looked behind me, no one was there, but when I looked back into the mirror, there he was. What a shock! I didn't believe that I would ever meet him again because I thought he had died the day I was delivered from Darkness. I closed my eyes and opened them again, but he was still there.

Manasseh started talking to me saying, "You and I are one and I am not going anywhere. I am in your body to stay and if I die, you die".

Things started to be wrong and abnormal again. It wasn't me again. I was double. One part of me was doing good things and the other part of me was doing bad things and people were saying it was me. I didn't argue because I knew I was double and not myself. Sometimes I was accused badly even though I was innocent. I didn't tell anyone because they would accuse me that I was not delivered.

I never gave up and I was determined not to go back to the Kingdom of Darkness. I told myself I would rather die in Christ Jesus and go to Heaven than to die in Darkness and go to Hell. No matter what tricks the devil tried to play to get me back, I overcame them.

As for Manasseh, I fasted and prayed against all the covenants I had with Satan including the blood covenant I had made with him. After that, Manasseh died and I was delivered from Satanic bondage, totally set free by the power of Jesus Christ, the son of the most high God.

Despite everything that had happened, prophetess Dinah taught me the word of God. She taught me how to pray. I also learned to speak with and listen to the Holy Spirit. Through her teaching I was able to grow spiritually into a strong, mature Christian who can now claim her rights in Christ Jesus. I now enjoy the Liberty of Salvation. If you ever meet me and see me happy, it is the joy of salvation by Jesus Christ, the son of God, who took all the punishment of my sins away and made me whole again.

One day I was watching TV when something strange happened to me. The TV went blank. I started speaking in tongues of the heavenly language in the Holy Spirit. I received the gift to speak in tongues in that moment and I was baptized with Holy Spirit. My spiritual eyes opened. I was taken to a place in the spirit. I saw the sections of the place and every corner of that place.

I saw an accident that was about to occur where people would die in that accident. Then I heard a small voice telling me to stand up. The voice told me to command a stop to the accident and if I didn't, the blood of their salvation would be required from my hands. The voice told me that I must follow a light that I will see to a place and that I will be the only person who will be seeing it. When I arrive there, I must pray against the accident occurring. I did. As I stood there praying in a manner that no one noticed, a truck came and hit another truck. By the grace of God, no one died. There were just a few minor injuries to a few people.

The following week on Friday, around 23:30, I was home from church with Prophetess Dinah. Inside the house I started to feel a strong, strange heat. I went to sit down outside the house. While I was sitting there observing the atmosphere, I saw fire surrounded by mist-like clouds. I didn't bother to go and tell the prophetess what I saw. I was interested in knowing the origin of the fire and where it was going. I went outside the gate of her yard. The fire was coming towards me. It came close and I heard a voice coming from it saying, "Let's go". I quickly ran to the house and told the prophetess what had happened. She didn't even bother to ask question of where and how. She just said, "God". When I went outside again, that cloud of fire overshadowed me.

After a while I appeared in another world where I saw very beautiful grass that I've never seen before in my life. I saw sheep grazing. They were fat and fresh. I saw a very large building that was shiny everywhere. Next to a certain building they were sheep that were thin. I saw a man close to them who was holding a rod who looked like a Shepherd.

I saw a building with unending steps. In front of it, angels were flying up and down singing songs that

I couldn't understand. While I stood there, a man appeared and said, "Ledia, never give up until you've fulfilled your destiny and have arrived where God wants you to reach". He then spoke about the sheep I saw.

He said, "Do you see the sheep that are grazing by themselves? They don't have a Shepherd who can take them to the river to drink water. They don't even change the place where they are grazing, but they are fat. Look at the other sheep that have a shepherd, but they are thin."

He said, "This is what it means: The sheep represent the people in the churches; the green grass represents wealth. Those sheep that don't have Shepherds or a Shepherd near them are just by themselves. In churches today people just go there with intentions to get wealth from God as well as the ability to make money. They enjoy the wealth in their closet. They forget that they don't have Shepherd. They have forgotten that they can get lost because they don't have someone to lead them. Their riches make them forget that there is God, who is a Shepherd. The church means Heaven. They don't know the meaning and the difference between Going to Church and Being a real Christian. They follow riches. Those people are lost. They don't know that the Holy Spirit is out of their churches.

Because they benefit on what is not theirs, they are rich physically, but poor spiritually".

He then continued: "The thin sheep represent people who worship God in spirit and in truth. They look poor in the eyes of man, but are rich in spirit. These people will enter Heaven because they have the one and only Shepherd who will show them the way. They are filled with the Spirit of the Most High, waiting for the most high to bless them. They don't follow the ways of man to make riches. They are the ones with the fear of the Lord and are not afraid of the schemes of the wicked. They are patient like a farmer who waits for the due season to reap the harvest".

That was my experience with God, incidentally.

Brothers and sisters, I've suffered a lot in my life. Jesus took my burdens away. People hated me so much after my deliverance. They hated me so much. I was always accused of doing things that I didn't do. My friends rejected me and abandoned me as well. The Devil also tried to make me kill myself.

To other Devil worshippers, there is nothing that Lucifer will offer you. The only mission he has is to kill, to steal and to destroy. He will use you and dump you and if you have bad luck, he will dump you in Hell for eternity. Bonds and covenants you made with Satan can only be broken if first you receive Jesus Christ as your Lord and Savior and second you repent genuinely from your sins.

Our clock usually runs faster than God's clock. We expect him to fulfill all his promises according to our schedule. God has a timetable for everything and his Kingdom doesn't appear all at once. God's best is worth waiting for. Patience brings its own reward of peace.

The Devil is a liar. I've made my confession and am still alive. You won't die if you confess everything and expose the Kingdom of Darkness.

Satan is a murderer. For those who obey him, he lies to them, steals from them, destroys them and kills them. That is his mission: to kill, to steal and destroy.

For you are the children of your father the devil, and you love to do the evil things he does. He was a murderer from the beginning. He has always hated the truth, because there is no truth in him. When he lies, it is consistent with his character; for he is a liar and the father of lies. **John 8:44.**

But Jesus came that we might have life abundance as well as to redeem us from our committed sin that has separated us from God our creator, the almighty God.

The thief's purpose is to steal and kill and destroy. My purpose is to give them a rich and satisfying life. **John 10:10.**

If you are a person who is under Satan's Dark Kingdom, whatever the Devil has promised you is a myth. As well, his promises are temporary. Why risk your eternity in Hell for a temporary gift that he offers. Repent and accept Jesus who has life eternal. He has paid for the most we need. You ask and you will receive. God has promised through Jesus Christ that we live for eternity in a place where Jesus will take us, where there is no sorrow or pain, where even Satan will not be found.

Then I saw a new heaven and a new earth, for the old heaven and the old earth had disappeared. And the sea was also gone. **Revelation 21:1**

Explanation of the Satanic Symbols

A Pyramid

The sign of the pyramid is so dangerous because it is from the Kingdom of Darkness. There are pastors who get power from the underworld located in the rivers. For some of them, the Queen of the Sea gives them the power to draw many people to their churches. The Queen gives them rings and a chain that has a sign of this pyramid as a form of initiation. The ring is called a pyramid ring. The Kingdom of Darkness brings this ring to our real world. Those who use them to get married unwarily can often experience marital problems until they divorce because for marriage it is designed as a curse, not a blessing.

A Satanic Bible (Brilho Celeste)

"Brilho Celeste" means, "Holy Bible" in a satanic language and in the view of those in the Satanic Kingdom of Darkness. The Satanic Bible was designed in the Kingdom of Darkness. The outer cover is just like any true bible of God. On the cover page is written "Brilho Celeste". The cover page has a cross with a snake on it. The difference between the Satanic Bible and the true Holy Bible is that the Satanic Bible has everything written the opposite of that in the Holy Bible. For example Matthew 6:10 says: "Our father who art in heaven...etc.".

Opposing the Holy Bible in the Satanic Bible it is written: "Our father who art on earth Hallowed be thy name… etc.".

You have to pray for the spirit of discrimination so that you can be able to differentiate between these bibles. The danger of the Satanic Bible is that if you're not filled with the spirit of God and if you open it and read it, you become possessed with evil spirits, demons and devils.

An Evil Eye

The evil eye occurs when you're a person who is under Satan or the Kingdom of Darkness. Whether you know you're in the Kingdom of Darkness or not, it watches you wherever you go. It might be at work, school or anywhere. When the evil eye is looking you, you won't concentrate on anything. You imagine accidents happening; you crave for blood. Your brain is overpowered with evil thoughts. You might be in Darkness unaware. Dreaming bad or evil things can be one of the signs that you're a victim.

Reversed Cross (Upside Down Cross)

The Satanic cross is upside down. Consider the cross on which Jesus was crucified. If it were turned upside down, Jesus' legs would be up and His head down. That's how the Satanic cross is turned to be opposite of the way the cross of Jesus was. According to the Holy Bible, the cross represents defeat over sin and Satan. The upside down Satanic cross represents or is a symbol of Saint Peter, the first Pope. The legend is that he was crucified upside down to show that he was not worthy of dying the same way that Jesus did. It serves as a symbol of people under Satan. In general in the Kingdom of Darkness, it is a sign and symbol that that person with the symbol has embraced Satan and rejected Jesus and has embraced the reversed cross symbol.

Sigil of Baphomet
The Sigil of Baphomet is the official symbol of the church of Satan that is located in the United States of America. It is used in organizations that have association with Satan or the Kingdom of Darkness. The Baphomet has to do with a satanic goat formed by Eliphas Levi. On the satanic goat head, one horn represents evil and the other one good. Sigil of Baphomet means association with Satan.

The 666
In the New Testament, the number 666 represents the number of the beast, the dragon, the old serpent, which is Satan. It is a widely recognized symbol of the antichrist or alternatively the Devil as mentioned in the Christian bible.

Satanic Tattoos Symbols and their Significance

You can be serving Satan while not knowing it. Tattoos are the key ways and the doorway for Satan and his demons to use you any way they want. Tattoos have satanic power associated with them and the Most High God has warned us of them:

You shall not tattoo yourself or make any craven image upon your body, nor cut gashes in your body to mourn for the dead. **Leviticus 19:28.**

Tattoos are associated with the Kingdom of Darkness, demons and evil spirits, as well as blood covenants. Here are the interpretations of the ones to which I was exposed as a Devil Worshipper:

1. *A Reversed Cross Tattoo.* It is a sign and that you have rejected Jesus and embraced Satan.

2. *A 666 Tattoo*: It is the mark of the beast. Once you have this mark on you, you're allowed to have access to all the things of the Kingdom of Darkness. As well, it is a sign and symbol that you belong to Satan.

3. *A Grave Tattoo:* When you have a grave tattoo, it means you are used to dig graves and to take dead bodies to the Devil.

4. *A Broken Heart Tattoo:* It is used to plant hatred in a person. Having it means that you have embraced hate.

5. *A Snake Tattoo:* If you're a lady it might be used against you to prevent you from ever giving birth. If you're a man, you'll find pleasure only when people fight and blood is shed.

6. *A Frog Tattoo:* It is used to plant the spirit of drunkenness, to make the person with it a heavy drinker.

7. *A Fish Tattoo:* It represents the Queen of the Sea, the mermaid underworld satanic spirit. It gives her the ability to possess you through that tattoo and use you for any of her missions.

8. *A Spider Tattoo:* Anyone who has this tattoo becomes recruited to Satan. It is also used as a trap by Satan. If you have this tattoo, you are allowing yourself to fall into the trap of Satan.

9. *A Scorpion Tattoo*: It represents the red
   gown of Darkness. As well, it is a sign that
   you have killed many people. In the
   Kingdom of Darkness there are three
   gowns; white, red and black. If you wore
   the white one, it is a sign that you've just
   joined Darkness and you haven't killed
   anyone. If you wore the red one, it is a sign
   that you've killed many people. If you
   wore a black gown, it is a sign that you
   killed someone of your blood, a family
   member or a relative of yours.

10. *A Pig Tattoo*: It means that you've built
    houses in the Kingdom of Darkness or
    houses for those who completed their
    Devilish missions.

11. *A Skull Tattoo*: It represents death or
    mortality.

12. *A Butterfly Tattoo*: It represents adultery,
    fornicator as well a prostitute and a
    cheater.

The tattoos are so many. Tattoos are used in the
Kingdom of Satan, the Kingdom of Darkness.
Tattoos are evil. Every form of a tattoo is a key or

doorway for the Devil to operate using that person with a tattoo. You can observe the character of people with tattoos. Some are prostitutes, murderers, armed robbers, drug dealers and so on.

Upside Down Pentagram and a Snake with Seven Heads

A reverse red pentagram with two points pointing upwards is a symbol of evil and it attracts sinister forces. It also represents the goat used to attack other forces in the heavenly realms.

A snake with seven heads is one that belongs to Satan and the Kingdom of Darkness. The seven heads of that snake carry seven crowns with these symbols on each of the different heads:

- 666
- Three Evil Eyes
- Money
- Crossed fingers
- Pyramids symbol
- Satanic Bible
- A Queen or King with a crown.

Brethren, on which side are you? Are you with Jesus or Satan? In the Kingdom of Darkness or the Kingdom of Light?

Jesus loves you with a great love. His salvation is a celebration that brings joy into our lives. He brings healing unto our bodies and peace into our lives.

Satan was defeated on Calvary when Jesus died. His blood was shed as a sacrifice for the remission of our sins as well as forgiveness for the punishment of our sins.

Thank you for reading my confession.

God Bless You.

I pray for you that may you miss Hell and not miss Heaven.

God bless you.

See you in heaven one day.

Don't forget: God loves you with a great love.

Shalom!

William Jenkins, Publisher
This activity was started in 2014 for the purpose of self-publishing mystery-adventure stories that are supplementary reading for elementary school students (about Grade 5). The titles as follows:

The Case of the Ancient American
The Case of the Brainy Birds
The Case of the Cannabis Cat
The Case of the Diligent Detectives
The Case of the Electrified Envoy
The Case of the Forgotten Fort
The Case of the Greedy Goat
The Case of the Hidden Hound

Mr. Jenkins edits and publishes stories submitted to him.

See http://williamjenkins.ca for details on this free service.

Mr. Jenkins can be contacted at:

williamhenryjenkins@gmail.com

Mr. Jenkins will send you a free copy of one of his stories in PDF format upon request.

Set Free From Satanic Bondage